Daydreams *and* Midnight Realities

Daydreams *and* Midnight Realities

A Collection of Poetry, Prose, Short Stories and Haiku

MOHAMMED ABRAR AHMED

First published by Mohammed Abrar Ahmed 2019

Copyright © 2019 by Mohammed Abrar Ahmed

All rights reserved. No part of this publication may be reproduced, stored or transmitted in any form or by any means, electronic, mechanical, photocopying, recording, scanning, or otherwise without written permission from the publisher. It is illegal to copy this book, post it to a website, or distribute it by any other means without permission.

First edition

ISBN: 978-0-9979824-9-7

Email: theficklepoet@outlook.com

*To the friends who believed in me, to 'HF'
who will always be the one and 'Hamza'
who made me want to finish this.*

I love you all.

Contents

Foreword 13
Acknowledgement 15

I: Falling in Love

Blank Pages 19
The Chaos in my Life 20
Warnings 22
When I Fall 23
Visions of the Future 24
Thunderstorms 25
In that Moment 26
Scars 27
Mistakes 28
December 29
Lost 30
4:11 AM - Story 31
6:00 AM 32
Loneliness 33
3:05 AM 34
Losing 36
Unspoken Tales 37
Brilliance 38
What Am I? 39

Why do we Love? 40
Pictures 41
Choices. 42
The Traveler 43
I Still Love 'Her' 44
Keep Distance. 45
Echo 46
Time. 47

II: The Journey

The Life – Before 51
The Life – After 52
The Day 53
The Night. 54
Indecisiveness 55
An Imaginary Proposal 56
The Tremor 58
Monday 59
After Effects. 61
Tears. 63
Apologies. 64
Common Ground. 65
No Interaction. 66
Too Busy for Love. 67
Life Support. 68
Friends. 70
Cold 72
The Rain and the Tears 73
Forgetting the Unforgettable. 75

Need to Know	76
The Dead Face	77
Improvised	78
The Secret	79
Revelation	80
Questions	81
Answers	82
Everyone Knows	83
Life Now	84
Indestructible	85
27 Years	86
Broken	87
The First Contact	88
Where is She?	89
Losing "Her"	90
Moving On	91
The Anchor	93
Do You Know?	94
It's Not the End	95
Loneliness II	96
Depression	97
The Push	98
Closure	99
Not Yet	100
We Are	101
Left	103
Collateral Damage	104
Life's Lesson	105
There	106
Regrets	108

Life Support II....................................109
What We Said 110
Morphine...111
What 'He' Craves 112
My Existence.....................................114
Road to You......................................115
What if?...116
Love at First Sight...............................117
I Know 118
Sleeping Beauty..................................119
Last Breath......................................120
The Stranger in the Mirror 121
One Day..122
Once in a Lifetime 123
A Memory in Description..........................124
Broken II 125
Life's Journey...................................126
Broken Souls.....................................128
Nights as These..................................129
Losing it Finally 131
Pain is the Fear 132
Seasons..133
The Push 135
New Year's Eve 136
The Healer.......................................137
Love's Destruction 138
Distant..140
She Will be Loved................................141
It's About Love 142
What He Had to Offer.............................143

Do You Remember?..............................144
Unclaimed Love 146
The Pull......................................148
What Love Is?.................................149
Within Me.....................................150
Hope..151
Almost..152
Mine..153
Warm You Up...................................154
Questions as These............................155
Blurry..156
Last Will.....................................157

III: The End Begins

Silence 161
Always 162
Scattered 163
Cold 164
May Be..165
Universes.....................................166
Hold This Heart 167
Drowned 168
Tripping......................................169
Journey.......................................170
Death 171
Waiting.......................................172
Porcelain Snow 173
Unleash the Soul..............................174
No Way Back...................................175

Jar of Regrets	176
Renaissance	177
Revival	178
The House I Was Born	179
Starting Anew	180
Stumble	181
12:45 (08-05-2019)	182
About the Author	184

Foreword

I was very reluctant to write a foreword for Abrar. Mostly because I have known him and been friends with him for a long time now. A touch biased, it's sometimes difficult to separate the man from the poet. Abrar is a remarkable person. Having known him for the last 8 years, I have never been more in awe of his strength of character and mind. To say that he has constantly fought fate is an understatement. Devoid of triviality, supportive friend, giving and touching peoples lives through his poetry is what he does best. Skillfully weaving pain, love, laughter – the dark and the light – he creates a masterpiece of words. To know his poetry is to know him.

This book is exceptional. What distinguishes it from others is the outpouring of feelings that is an undeniable part of it. Fiction and non-fiction merge together to give an account of life experiences. Experiences that we take for granted or overlook but which are etched and honed to perfection by an imaginative and arcadian mind. Done with a skill that draws you in and a simplicity that touches your heart.

For those of us who read poetry simply to enjoy it, this book will do that just. He uses his gift to make poetry so much more comprehensible and unlocks an often-indecipherable world.

I am honored to know Abrar as a friend and I am privileged to be able to witness the magic he does on paper. He inspires me and he teaches me – as a friend and as a poet.

-Rachael Linda Lewis

Acknowledgement

Thank you Al-Mighty for blessing me with everything in my life and all of you for your constant support.

I

Falling in Love

Blank Pages

I try every night to fill these pages
with the description of your perfect
face, yet the only thing I see is
the pointer taunting at me and saying
you'll never do it. I try waiting all
night for the words to make their
way onto paper, I call and sing
nothing but your name and all I
can add with it is the word "beautiful."

These blank pages are going to be
filled only with your name and
the world would still be able to
read what I've always wanted to say.
My every thought, covered with
the highest respect during the day,
and every thought undressed
under the moonlight. Even, after
everything is inked in black
on these white pages, they'd still
be blank. These pages need your
touch for words to show, and
just like me, they're waiting too…

The Chaos in my Life

She is a storm amidst the calm,
a wonderful woman, a warrior, a survivor
a fierce lover.
I've been able to calm her
to fold her wings
which are ever ready to fly
away at the slightest
inconvenience. She had
asked me to leave and I stayed.
She asked me to die and meant it
and I lived, for her. With her.
She loves me, not the kind
where there's kisses and hugs,
but the kind which shares pain,
her eyes, black with glooming darkness
searching for light.
She has life figured out,
she has love figured out.
she is different, but looks
the same. Flesh and bones,
she is. It hurts to hurt her.
She cries, she whispers, when she
says 'I love you' and she hugs
like you've been missing from her

The Chaos in my Life

for centuries. Her back smooth as
milk cream and tastes like strawberries.
I kiss her and put her to sleep,
she never lets me leave,
She says 'no' like an innocent child,
and her anger is never mild.
She's a warrior. It's either her way
or no way. I love her. This chaos
of a person, she asks me why
every time I tell her that.
And the answer to that is,
I've always loved nature and
hurricanes are my favorite
and sweet heart you are one hell
of a hurricane.

Warnings

She warned him
It was going
to get crazy.

He knew
that wasn't
going to stop
him from falling
for her.

When I Fall

I've been constantly
denied of happiness, and
love would never
stick around.
Sorrow stayed.
Loneliness was
the only companion.

Then I met you,
and here I am,
thirty thousand
feet above the
ground flying home,
and though I am alone
amidst the people
I don't really know,
I'm content, happy,
even if I fall
towards the ground,
there's someone
who'll catch me.

Visions of the Future

I see beyond the darkness
at the end where light begins,
where there's no place for hate
and only love remains.
There are no bombs anymore,
lives are valued
like they mean something,
like they mean everything.
There are no refugees,
the land belongs to everyone.
There are no labels attached
to religion and there's no children
dying of starvation.
I see a future that sees
how blind it has been in the past.

Thunderstorms

Watching out of my bedroom window,
raindrops rolling down and fade.
A cup of coffee in my hand and
memories in mind, so very vague.

Of all the things I could not say,
of all the things I could not do,
sitting here thinking of you,
makes me wonder what we would do.

There's a thunderstorm outside now
trying to pull us in with its might.
It's been too long since I have said this,
for too long you've been out of sight.

In that Moment

I found myself lying that I am strong; I cannot feel pain or emotions like love or hate, which sounds more like an ugly fate. And then I found out that this is a world where words are strangled and used as bait. You don't know who you fall in love with, when or why you do the things that you are doing, but the feeling is overwhelming and you want to feel this way forever and before you know it, in that moment you are bound by something which doesn't even exist.

In that moment look for a place, cover yourself up and fight this feeling, which isn't there. Love, in all its might is a warrior who kills the heart, rip the soul, and gives lives to those who are longing for it. When you feel love, hate, sorrow, or joy, just remember you are open and bound to get hurt, which is the most beautiful pain you will ever bear. Those moments you will never get, it's a fight for freedom, your freedom. Close your eyes and let go of it. In that moment, nothing else matters and it's just you and a fight for your needs with your wants. Choose needs, love will find you, and when you are heart-struck and in pain, remember to close your eyes and let go of this pain, because once you do, there is no pain in it, but joy, and you are in that moment forever free.

Scars

Silent nights, deafening noise
loneliness, love ignites
winter pains, dreadful time
unheard sigh, feelings die
Then there is a matter of
what's true, what's a lie
with all that's happening
surprised I'm not paralyzed

She hears my unsaid sighs
ignores them, until my demise
with everything that has been
was I worth a sacrifice?
There's a mark on both our lips
which you couldn't understand,
we are stories intertwined we
have the perfect "Scars."

Mistakes

That's what we call them, not lessons, but mistakes.
And it kills me inside that I have been taught to look at it that way.

I stop looking at what lesson I learnt,
and focused more on finding out my mistake.

Where did I go wrong? Can that be corrected?

Mistakes can't be…

But lessons…
They can be learnt,
and applied
and you win for sure.
Fail, learn and apply…
Make mistakes!
And forgive yourselves once in a while for making them.

December

The cold touch of air on my skin,
those feelings tied up deep within.
you search for a meaning
dreaming of something,
which will never be.

Among the many things, that life has given me
I always find something to be missing
deep within my shadow haunts me
there's nothing about life to be reminiscing

In my solitude, I sit thinking of a kiss
which you and I haven't shared yet.
I feel a cold touch on my hands
opened my eyes to see, but there's nothing

It's just the season of Love,
it's the December winds hissing.

Now I know all this while,
it was you I have been missing.

Lost

"With every passing moment I lose a part of me which I might never find,

I lose it in search of you and if I could never find you I might one day be completely lost."

4:11 AM - Story

"Just passing by and saying hello
does not mean you care.
You sometimes have to turn and smile."

6:00 AM

"It's 6 am and I still can't sleep,
the visions of you keep me awake."

Loneliness

"When you are lonely and nothing seems to go your way, there isn't any magical place in this world that you can find comfort. Sure, you can try to smile for some time hoping everything turns right but deep down you know it won't resolve anything, the only thing you need is effort to make things work in your favor.

The only magical place which exists is in the arms of your lover or something or someone that you really want, which you have to go out and get it against all odds. In the end, your persistence, and love for the person or the thing you want the most matters and that's the most magical feeling you will ever get!"

3:05 AM

Well, here we are. The clock is ticking, it's very late, and I cannot sleep. I thought of writing poetry but some thoughts have taken captive the best of me. I am getting old; and watching the clock tick, as growing old wasn't on my to-do list. This emptiness with the whole world in it doesn't make it seem empty any more. If you listen carefully there is something whispering in the sheer silence, a thought in your head, running all the scenarios you ever thought could happen to you in the middle of the night. Maybe tonight's the night. Maybe it is not. Maybe all of this is in my head and I am asleep. When did life become so full of maybe and what ifs?

Maybe I don't have a great future, at least that's the way it seems with me in the driver's seat. But like I said there are what ifs always surrounding us. What if there is a turn which I may not be aware of? What if that turn will start to set events of my life in motion, which I have been waiting for? Why can't I sleep? Could there be an explanation for all this? Will she talk to me again? *SHE..* No matter how hard I try, she makes her way in my thoughts. I have shut the door on her face so many times, yet she is always in. It's like magic. I told my friends about

3:05 AM

this. They laughed at me. They say I need to let her go. To be honest I never had her, just so you know.

I cannot leave her out of what I write, because she is what I write. A thousand different scenarios playing in my head, what she must be doing at this moment? Is she safe? Does she think of me too? How do we meet again? That's it. That's the answer isn't it? How do we meet AGAIN? (Yes, I know it's a question, but couldn't that be an answer). Maybe, what if the turn in my life is when we meet again? That would end so much suffering. However, I don't know the answer to the trickiest question of all: *WHEN?* Sure as hell it isn't tonight.

Losing

"It's stupid how we lose ourselves for someone we know for such a short time. We don't know what they want from their future but start hoping to be in it. Like there is no one else in this world you will ever fall for. Well, I am that stupid too. But I don't think I can wait any longer. When someone says, you didn't wait and you said you love her/him, that's what chips me out. I lose it. I admit there is a time in our lives where we fall for someone whom we are not meant to be with. You can wait all your life if there is an expression from the other person that they want you to wait. Is there?

No. There has never been. People who love someone but they don't love you back, kills you every day on the inside. It rips you open. It makes you vulnerable. Don't let that happen. You deserve love. You deserve more. You deserve better. Keep saying this until you believe it. Let go of the things that bring you down. (Unless you are mid-air and hanging onto a ledge or something don't take this advice). We all deserve good things/people/love, which care for us as much as we do."

Unspoken Tales

"It's been months, yet I have still saved your footprints in the room under the staircase. Hoping one day, you would mistakenly drop by and I would return them to you.

I had seen you today after months. That face of yours, which wasn't as much glowing, as it is today; when he had left you to be with someone else and that's when I met you. Didn't know what your story was. That vivacity on your face during that time was like that I had never seen before. Fell in love with you in an instant and proposed to you the next. What was I thinking?

Well, your face is more radiant now than it was then. I heard the guy who left has come back in your life again. I kept looking at you for a long time. But you didn't look back.

Or did you?"

Brilliance

"Saw her from the corner of my eye,
didn't know what to say
as we have not spoken in a very long time.

She caught me looking at her (as she always does)
and I look away as I get caught.
It was different this time.

Her face seemed brighter than the sun
yet as soft as the moonlight.
It was not the beauty in her that mesmerized me.
It was her brilliance that caught my eye."

What Am I?

What am I? An unheard scream, a wishing machine,
unfulfilled dreams, a mother's hope,
father's stick, a sister's need, my family's pride…

What am I?

Unspoken tale, which has been said a million times and forgotten,
a dream, dreamt a hundred times with open eyes,
an ocean, whose waves pull me down when I come up,
a desert, who does not know the way out of its own,
a cry, in the middle of the night alone walking home,
or a shadow, which seems to be there without a soul…

What am I?
I am what I need to be free,
I am the rain to wash my tears off when I cry,
I am the seed you need to sow,
I am the wreck you left to die,
I am what I am because I survived…

Why do we Love?

Why do we love? The answer to this question is the same as to the question: Why do you love him/her? And that answer is: …

It's unknown, why we fall for people we don't even know and when they become so important part of our lives. What's known about love is that it can happen with any one in an instant or over a period of time and leave you to be the most vulnerable and miserable person on the face of this planet if you don't get the tiniest bit of love back from the person you admire.

The sad part is she understands this,
but doesn't feel the same for me.
I guess that's what being in love means.

Pictures

"I keep looking at your pictures every day, hoping someday they will say all the things you never did. I keep hoping they would finish the conversations we never got a chance to start."

Choices

"I am the reflection of the choices I make,
the decisions to let go or hold on.
I am me because I am strong enough to breathe."

The Traveler

"I travel from time to time and fall in love with total strangers hopelessly. It sort of breaks my heart that we can never be together, and that gives me the satisfaction that I can still feel something."

I Still Love 'Her'

"There's something about the morning sun today, it does not burn anymore. I guess this is what I was waiting to see; the clouds and the rain could make everything cold but could not put out the fire burning within me for her. I guess this is why I still love her. I love her more than the sun loves the earth."

Keep Distance

"I've said it before, I will say it again.
Stay away from me, lest you want to fall
on the shattered pieces of my heart, hurt yourself,
and be driven away from me for the rest of eternity.
Or you can just watch me suffer and be!"

Echo

"The echo of her voice resonates in my head. She had lost love and I found it in her. If only regret didn't exist, I wouldn't have told her how I felt.

She turned me down in a second, not wanting to know what I needed. I clung onto the self-destruct feeling for a year, before finally understanding that things you love hurt you more than things you know are bad, and will eventually hurt you. At least they cause the pain and leave. Love just keeps hurting even after everyone's dead.

The irony of your choice."

Time

I see three clocks ticking in my living room, all show a different time. I walk past by one which is running ten minutes late and then the next which is five minutes fast and then there's the clock which stopped years ago. In a moment I was ten minutes in the past and five minutes in the future to the moment where time had stopped. I put my hand in my pocket pull out the phone to see myself in present again. I can't change or foresee anything but I can stay in this moment where the present is in my hand and stopped on my wall clock…

II

The Journey

The Life – Before

Carefree and fun, as it used to seem,
there was a time as though it was a dream,
I woke up to find out that, it was all a lie,
I lived a life of mistakes and sighs…

Here I am looking in my past,
to find a moment, to surpass,
this feeling I hide deep inside,
is this the way true love ignites?

I am looking in the corners
of my empty room
to find a spot, of my eventual doom,
does it even matter now if I succumbed?

As hard as it may seem to believe,
I truly want to end here this folklore,
I laid my eyes on you and for me,
It's impossible to resume *The Life – Before*…

The Life – After

I can't distinguish a dream from reality,
I am losing my sense of morality,
I daydream now, Oh! My eyes are open,
this cannot be cupid's dreaded token…

I look for you in the halls and near the staircase,
and when found, you pass with a straight face,
have I totally lost my senses?
did you notice? I am defenseless completely…

I stammer when I talk,
then I completely stalk,
I say Hi with a smile,
then catch my breath for a while…

These are not isolated incidents,
I don't see any other end to this,
I dreamt us standing at the Altar,
just to clarify, it's *The Life – After*…

The Day

It had been a long time, me being away from this place, and today I have returned. I see new faces everywhere and some old relations too. I had no clue what had changed and who had come and gone because it never bothered me any way. All I did was notice. I thought this day would be the same as rest and I would just do what's needed to be and leave.

Life is never so simple; I had no clue things were going to change forever. I did not think twice that I could spend the whole night up in trying to describe her innocence in words.

I tried, tried, and later failed miserably to keep my eyes off her the day I saw her standing right in front of me. I like to think I did go home that night, but I knew…

I had left something behind…

The Night

Here I am, laid back in my bedroom trying to forget everything I had felt today. Still trying to calm down all the senses in my body. I know it's not possible until I tell her how I feel about her and that's the tricky part.

I don't know how to do that.

I went through all the proposals I had ever seen in every movie and still couldn't find the best way to do so. The best way I thought was just to go ahead with it without thinking about any consequences.

Never thought I will regret the decisions made that night forever. Some way life just happens to all of us and all we can do is just go with its flow. Flowing against the current has dire consequences.

I guess I will learn it the hard way...

Indecisiveness

To say or not to say. It's all I have in my
head for the past couple of days and its killing me.
I muster up the courage as though it's a war to be
fought and I know I was on the losing end.
I know I should not be talking about this
with any one as this could ruin everything for me.
I keep this secret and don't say a word to any one…

Until it's too late.

An Imaginary Proposal

Well this is what it comes down to. This day will be the end of all the misery I have been in for the past couple of weeks. The world I knew ceased to exist and I am finally going to tell her how I feel about her.

I requested her to meet under the staircase at the back. There isn't any better place to do it, you just have to say it right. Well that's what I had thought and to my surprise she showed up. That's when it started.

Jitters in my body and not being able to say a word in her presence. I put my hand in my pocket to take out the letter I wrote in case my voice gave up on me, irony there, I froze completely. I mustered up the courage and spoke to her finally, "I love you", I said. And that's what she had expected, with me being all jittery and trembling. I look at her waiting for a response and there it was, "I am sorry" (At this point there was no going back for me, I knew exactly where this was leading).

"I like your honesty but a relationship is not what I am seeking".

An Imaginary Proposal

She didn't have a problem with the "Love You" part, she just didn't like "I" before it. It was clear she loved "Him" but not "I" and "He" was with someone else at the time. I just couldn't get over the irony of the situation. The irony of "I" and "You". The love part just stays until it doesn't any more.

Those were the last words I heard that night. She turned around and in an instant was out of sight. I looked up, there she was looking down through the window. Looked as if she was checking up on me after a hard blow.

I just looked silently, words lost, thrown back. This was me being love struck which never turned into romance...

The Tremor

I was alone, standing in the dark,
with remorse that I lost my only shot,
trembling with fear that I messed up everything,
I knew it was the end of a new beginning…

I felt heartbroken; it took the best of me,
how could I sit back and let life play me?
It was the thing I needed then the most,
I had no clue I was just playing the host…

It starts to rain and drenches me completely,
I stand without a feeling, somebody move me,
that was the time I remembered too clearly,
you love in life what doesn't love thee…

It was about time, I moved from the place,
for one night in couple minutes, lots been misplaced,
my heart beats with a slow sound of murmur,
I hold my hand with the other to control *the tremor*…

Monday

There are times in our life we are so adamant about the things we want that we refuse to take "no" for an answer. Somewhere along the line, I made the same mistake and I don't have a clue how to correct it. Life's simple pleasures are in making someone you love happy and nothing else seems to matter if you accomplish that.

I have indeed misread a situation and went rogue at it hands down and chin up. I think of the day, that Monday, when the consequences of my actions were revealed to me. I still could not forget her red eyes, which of course were due to relentlessly crying. I could see clearly those tears in her eyes and immediately moved away from in front of her. I sure did remind her of someone. Perhaps someone she loved and lost.

They say when you love someone tell them. It's better to live a life filled with 'oh wells!' than 'what ifs?' They never said, words of love could also be a source of pain for someone and you might end up regretting your whole life. For this instance, I would have chosen what if, I knew I would end up hurting her.

Well that's a tale about Monday which eventually ends on a Friday or so it seems...

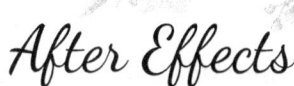

After Effects

This place I am at, I don't recognize it any more. Everything seems different and I could not recollect what was where and what has been moved. It hurts to breathe and I want to give up on life and end this misery forever. But that is not the solution; I know it and I have accepted it. I had always been a fighter and I will keep fighting this feeling until the end of eternity, just to come on top of this.

I have started avoiding eye contact with people I know, the only reason is that they know me and can contemplate that something is off with me and I would have to tell them if they insisted. So I just say Hi and move on. I have taken additional work to keep myself busy and spend almost eighteen hours in office so when I go home; I will be tired enough that I fall asleep as soon as I crash on my bed. But you know, that's not how this works.

That's not how any of this works.

I still think of you the remaining six hours without an ounce of sleep and drag myself to work the next day, hoping that today I will not think of you. Hoping that today, I will sleep.

I guess these are the After Effects of losing a battle you thought you could win easily.

Tears

The sky looks cloudy today, I remember distinctly about the time it looked this way. You would not, as you were not paying attention. I could smell the rain, the petrichor in the atmosphere. For a moment, I wished you were here with me, I know that's impossible now. I know your story. I try really hard to keep away but the harder I try the more our paths crossed. So I have given up on staying away.

There is this weight inside of me and I wish to get this off my chest. I want to talk to you or someone maybe. I want to apologize for falling in love with you. I wait for the rain to fall on the ground and get soaked in it, completely.

It was after many years, I felt this pain, this breathlessness. I could feel the tears rolling down my face in rain. I almost forgot that I have this tendency and it's because of you I was reintroduced to this feeling, this teary feeling that I was free of. Along with the rains, came the tears and I fall down to get up again.

And I do all this only to fool myself.

Apologies

It's the time of apocalypse,
just as in Greek mythologies.

Don't take this too hard,
don't start a hypothesis.

We are alone remember,
with closed parenthesis.

And if we survive this, love,
we will have *Apologies*.

Common Ground

We found a way to reunite,
with slow steps that astound,

when there was nothing,
there was surely your sound,

step by step, we came close,
and together formed a common ground.

No Interaction

Do you remember the old lady who used to live by the road, refusing to recognize anyone who came to meet her?

"Well, that's what loneliness does to you," she said.
"They meet once a year and act like I don't exist after they leave."

I don't want that to happen to us.

Too Busy for Love

Sometimes I give too much of my day away,
and sometimes too much of my night,
sometimes I just go down without a fight,

then some times
it is hard to contemplate,
if I were awake the whole day,
or was that the entire night?

Sometimes I don't have it in me
to stand tall and duck slight,
and finish the ongoing fight,
and sometimes I am the person
completely out of everyone's sight.

I don't mean to be disrespectful,
I clearly got some issues to resolve,
I am trying to redeem myself,
I am on the healing waterfall.

Now as helpless as I might look,
I had my fair share of life's shove,
lifted up, pressed down from above,
to enact, I am *too busy for love*.

Life Support

Have you ever been to a hospital? There are different proce-dures for different diagnoses. There are patients coding for whom they bring in the crash cart to revive them and then there are people who come in with hiccups and end up dead.

Then there are those who are fighting to live. They undergo surgery after surgery until they cannot anymore and understand that its time they stop the fight. People on life support tend to make doctors happy if they fight through and come out of it because they are breathing on their own now. They are safe.

Then there are those who fight and lose. They are comatose, brain dead or just lost the will to wake up, and they hurt the most. For them, life is a joy, which they are fighting to attain.

For some time now, I have been feeling plugged in to something or someone who does not even have any clue about my existence. I unintentionally made them my life support and I know this connection needs to be severed at some point in life, as this will only complicate things for me. We are not doctors, we are merely incapable people who cannot make the decision whether to let go or hold on. We make people our life support and threaten to take us off life if they let go of us.

Love demands to be the life support, it will kill you if you let go of it from your hearts.

Friends

Do you remember the hand extended to you when you were down? You didn't know who it was and where it might lead. You didn't know if it will it pick you up or leave you half way to fall again. In fact, you didn't know anything, however you held the hand anyway, hoping he or she will pick you up.

You trusted someone. You must have been in your initial phases of school, some person bullying you, you didn't know how to deal with them, and another person extending a hand at that time is probably the one who you trusted after your parents and teachers.

That was the start of a new relationship: Friendship. You may or may not remain friends for a lifetime, but you always remember the name and deep down you know they were there for you when no one else was.

I have a few friends I miss and I don't know where they are anymore. They helped me through some very rough times. I miss them and I will always remember them.

We all have that one person who we confide in, be it anything.

This one is for all the Friends out there who were there to extend a hand when no one else was.

Cold

It's not about the weather,
or the adventures in store,
it's summer time right now,
what does the future hold?

A lost love in one hand,
a failed attempt at life,
a foggy question in head,
for whom do we survive?

We try to look for answers,
to fail again ridiculously,
far too many lost attempts,
which slowly and surely kills me…

I turned a new chapter to survive,
cut all my ties as my life unfolds,
no reaction to happiness, sorrow, or pain,
I have turned into something *cold*…

The Rain and the Tears

Do you ever feel that when you are sad, somehow, everything around you looks sad? For some reason, all the things, people, nature... They all just look sad. I know there's no logical explanation to all this, probably there is, which I haven't read or didn't come across yet.

You remember the time you could not stop crying because you loved a person so much, you couldn't be together for a reason, and it seemed like the end of the world for you. Nothing seemed to be right anymore; even when you were moving north, the south was pulling you.

Then you found that spot, your spot where you would sit alone for hours under the sky - blue, orange, sometimes red, and you remember that person, and hoping to be with them. You would give up anything to be with them in that moment and you know anything you can, giving up will not get them back or change their mind.

You haven't cried in a long time because you were strong for so long and you didn't want something as small as to love make you cry. However, you realized that's what you need, you burst into tears, and rain stars to fall on you at the same time, as if it's trying to comfort you and say you are not alone, I am sad for you too.

People find comfort in the most extraordinary places and that is all they need sometimes, a little solitude with The Rain and the Tears.

Forgetting the Unforgettable

I have turned cold mostly numb,
most of the time I sound dumb,
a moment in silence after another,
emptiness is what I seek to succumb…

There is a face that I keep drawing,
cold ice, which keeps thawing,
I notice what no one does,
I keep away from all the fuss…

I try to write what I call poetry,
your name keeps destroying my flow,
the thought of you, that I cannot lose,
this is surely going to kill me slow…

You don't know what I go through,
you have no idea what I am doing,
I will become what I call unstable,
All this is to forget the unforgettable…

Need to Know

Have you ever tried to guess what's really wrong with someone?

What makes them happy or sad?
Or
What makes them who they are?
Or
Why are they the way they are?

Have you ever felt that you
just need to know?

I don't need all the answers, I just need to know if you still think about me.

Or

Have you ever thought about me?

This I need to know, because I think of you as I write this.

I need to know.

The Dead Face

Another story for another time,
there is no drill to survive,
people ask all the time,
are you all right? Are you fine?

Take a step into the unknown,
come with me to the shore,
there's this emptiness in me,
somehow, I want you more…

A relativeness into the void,
hoping to know your darkest secrets,
I come home after many years,
people I know break into tears…

This is where I understand,
what everyone's been asking all along?
Another side effect of love misplaced,
I've been roaming around with *the dead face*…

Improvised

There is this emptiness, this void I am trying to fill with your memories. I am afraid, as I am running short of memories of you. I remember every time we spoke, shook hands, or looked at each other with a smile, and then we avoided each other without remorse. I remember how we met the first time and the events that followed that day. I remember all the details.

I have filled this void as much as I could but it's still half empty. My only option now is to fill it with the memories I have of our future together from my dreams. I have looked far too deep into the future, a future with you. Where you are always by my side and there's no losing you.

At this point I have improvised a love tale that does not exist, but one which keeps me hoping for a happy ending, eventually. At this point, you have become my muse...

The Secret

Do you remember how indecisive I was to tell anyone that I was in love?
I was hiding that secret all this time.

She knew, of course but no one else did.

Now everyone knows, but don't know who the person is.

I guess even after the secret is out, I still have something to protect.

I still have 'Her' to protect.

Revelation

I thought a lot about it and honestly, I cannot keep this within me any longer. I have said this a hundred times that I am so in love with you and I can say it hundred more times.

It's time for me to accept the fact that you will never love me. And I need to talk about this with someone who wouldn't judge me for falling in love with you.

It's time for revelation of the macabre that I have been hiding for so long behind this mask of a face that I am wearing. I need to feel something - the hurt, the loss of someone who meant the world to me, who still means the world to me, and someone who will never know. The air that sends chills down my spine in midst of dry summer, spells when I see you. This all comes down to you eventually and the part that hurts me the most is that you don't even know. And even if you did, you never acknowledged it.

So, here I am with this Revelation, that come what may I had loved you, I still love you and I will always love you...

I take it, you never saw this coming...

Questions

All I have with me are questions,
for which I strongly believe the answer is *you*…

However, the most important question is,
will you ever get to read this?

Answers

I still don't have the answers,
I still await your return…

However, this I have figured out by now,
that nothing lasts forever, only love does.

Everyone Knows

Do you remember that there was a secret to protect?

Well…

I

Don't

Anymore…

Everyone knows.

Life Now

I started with the life before,
then there was the life after,
a few scribbled pages and still,
don't know what the heart is after.

There was sheer fun,
there was the altar,
then some shattered dreams,
hanging from the ceiling beams.

Now the times are different,
and no one comes close to her,
left with no courage to take another vow,
this is the reality of life – *Life Now*.

Indestructible

I thought a lot and I have come to this conclusion,
that whatever I may say or do,
nothing will convince you more than
what I feel for you.

See, the feeling that I have for you,
is all I have and this feeling,
is indestructible.

27 Years

27 years have passed and I still don't have a clue where all this is headed. Nothing has changed. It still hurts how it used to earlier, it's just that I've learnt to ignore the pain or maybe got used to it. People who had said that I would be well settled, they have all been proven wrong. It's just that sometimes it takes more time. I will eventually get there.

27 years of fighting, falling on your face, picking yourself up, and moving forward is not a small task. Pat yourself once on the back. It's been a hell of a ride. I've had my fair share of experience in love and had my heart broken, no, shattered to a million pieces, yet I am here. I've failed tremendously, and sometimes won. I've said things I didn't mean and did things I didn't intend to. The best of all this is that I still don't have a clue what I am doing.

So, let this number 27, be the reminder. Reminder for the apologies made, friends gained, enemies lost, and affairs that ended before they even began. This is what I've survived. So, carry on, towards the next 27 to come. It's not going to be easy, however, it'll be worth it.

Broken

I started to pick up my broken pieces from the floor as I lay scattered and was afraid parts of me would be blown away with the wind. I somehow put myself back together and started to walk away from the place where my heart fell out of my chest and broke into a million pieces. I couldn't gather all of them but I managed to put together the part where you resided. It seemed like a wonderful idea at the time. Now I think it was a mistake. I cannot move on with this piece, clinging on to me.

I should've left that part there, but that was the biggest piece. I needed to put it back to survive. I chose my survival but you again came along. Don't you see how broken I am? Even with you residing in my heart. It's time you abandoned this place just the way you did when you turned away and left. I am already broken; I have the advantage this time. Leave; don't make me throw you out.

But wait, just tell me this, are you what's keeping me alive, even with all this damage?

The First Contact

After a month's absence, I finally came back. I left, not knowing or caring where the road will take me, or where I would end up, not knowing if I would ever return, nothing mattered any more. I just packed my bags and left to the first place that came to my mind. I ended up at your door twice, however, that was then. It doesn't matter anymore. I am back and I have to face it. I have to face you. I can't run away from you forever. Maybe I could but I don't want to any more.

I was walking in the corridor with these thoughts in my head and there you were, standing right in front of me. That was the first time I saw you after a month. All that alone time was for nothing. All those feelings for you, which I thought I had left behind came flooding back, how foolish of me to think that, this was a possibility. It never was. They just were suppressed, and came back as soon as I saw you.

I believe there are something's which no matter how hard we try to leave behind they don't let us go, they just are there waiting to be rekindled, waiting to consume us again.

I guess this is a new start for myself, or a new end. I just have to wait and find out myself.

Where is She?

Did you ever ask yourself this question? Where is she? Late during the night not able to sleep, thinking what had happened, where you are, and where she might be at this exact moment, or what she might be doing? Does it bother you not having all the answers your brain is seeking at this time, and all you need are answers because you are curious and you just want to know? Or maybe to understand if you still have a chance. I have asked this very question, until I started to question my very existence. I lost myself in this quest to know, or to understand why we love whom we love.

Listen to me, "I don't know if I will ever meet her again, all I have with me are some unspoken words which I never had the opportunity to say to her. I don't know if this feeling of regret ever fades away, but you surely will learn to smile and love again. Not in the same way, but you will. However, if you still have a chance, if you think you do, and you have her number, call her, don't look at the time just call and tell her how you feel. I didn't get the chance. If you have one, you take it. Trust me regret is something you don't want to live with. You don't want to live with this question for the rest of your life, do you?"

Losing "Her"

And from time to time I go over my mistakes, thinking what could have caused me to lose her. And every single time, I don't find myself the reason behind it. It's not me or her. It was the time. It was the universe, which had things written for us. Everyone calls it destiny; I call it the screw up.

I didn't have much to offer her then, nor do I have anything to offer now, the only thing that I have now are the words which I want to tell her and I can't. Words, which I started scribbling on paper over and over again, hoping that one day she will read them. This is what losing her has done to me.

I hope to get out of this alive, it doesn't look good, it never did…

Moving On

We all have loved, some of us found what we were looking for, and some are still in search of that one…

Then there are some, who have found the one. However, for innumerable reasons, cannot be with them, so they move on…

Then there are those who found that one, loved with all their hearts, knowing it will destroy their existence, but chose to do it anyway. They are the dreamers.

They are always referred to as the best that come but never stay. They are travelers, they love once, and that's all they need…

On the other hand, there are those who are patient, they wait, they love, and express it in the weirdest of times in unapologetic ways and they wait. They are honest to their being and they believe in one true love. They don't

Moving On

believe in moving on, because it is easy to say to move on but difficult to do so.

So, they wait until moving on is the only option…

Then they move on…

The Anchor

I tried it all: traveling, cooking, learning to play the guitar, poetry… Everything you could possibly think of that might help in getting my mind off you… Nothing ever really helped; I couldn't find the anchor which kept me close to you in my mind. I tried my best and the only thing that ever helped me was staying late at work…

I now realize that the only reason it helped was that you were there too. All the time, your presence kept me from destroying myself. You never knew this fact, but let me just say this, I always arrived before you and left after you did.

There was no anchor, except the work… That's the irony of life, it happens to you at the strangest of times. I am still trying to be acquainted to the fact that maybe I was wrong in loving you. Maybe, I am still wrong. But it feels right as ever, as always. And that is the reason I will continue to do so…

Do You Know?

I am not the sun or the moon, but I promise,
I can be everything in between.

I can be your friend when you need one
or your punchbag when you feel like picking up a fight
with someone.

I can be the stars at night and be the moon when
the sun comes up, still present with no trace of existence.

I can be what you want me to be, but the question is,
do you know what you want me to be?

Do you know what you really want?

It's Not the End

This is not the end, but this is the
beginning of something I am
yet to understand.
I have no clue what it is,
but I am certain that one day
I will see all the things you did
and question myself,
what was it that we couldn't notice all along?

Until then,
this just has to be the way it is.

Loneliness II

There is something
about loneliness,

you
always
tend
to
find someone
to share it
with…

Depression

It's been a year and half since I've said that I love you. This heavy feeling that I have in my heart I'm told will eventually subside and I will love again. However, no one has been able to answer how long it might take.

They don't call it by name, like it's something which takes over you if you name it. They just say she/he is feeling down. They are afraid to say, "She/he is depressed."

"Depression," it creeps up on you in solitude, and in the midst of people. There's no right or wrong time to come across it. It just plays out in its own time; to think you can control a human emotion is utterly the most ridiculous thing you will ever hear. You can't take your time, don't cut yourself, live it out. Come out stronger.

That's the only thing you can do when you are depressed. It has taken its toll on me in an unimaginable way, and one day you wake up and say to yourself that it's time to move on and you quit your job, buy some tickets, you travel until the moment it feels utterly right, and you start again. You smile again.

If you're smiling, it's over.

The Push

Standing on the edge of a cliff,
ready to throw it all away,
dreams of sleepless nights,
haunting you until this very day.

What lies beyond this great fall?
you take some time to think,
a speck of dust enters the eye,
and continuously you blink.

What will happen if you don't die?
take the fall and you still survive,
a speck of dust, you couldn't resist,
you lie half dead for vultures to feast.

Standing on the edge of a cliff,
you know it's a calculated risk,
do you want to feel the rush?
will you jump or do you need a push?…

Closure

Every day, regrettably is a different story for people like us…

People, who are all under the influence of love, are forgotten and deemed as crazy for taking the chances no one else dares to take, looking at things in a perspective that no one understands. We are tied loose and when the knot frees, we are lost forever into the oblivion and we re-surface in an unrecognizable weary situation with a varying smile.

In those times, we still give love the utmost respect even though it is the reason for this unimaginable pain that resides in our chest and travels to every part of the body determined to kill us in a soft agonizingly painful, loveless bed of death.

That's when we think that it would have been good, not great, to at least express the love that we have for someone, even though it might not work out…

I did try to tell her, and trust me, it doesn't give you the closure you've been seeking…

Not Yet

Please try to understand,
I didn't write this for you.
I wrote this for myself…

And me writing this,
doesn't mean
I am actually going through it.

I may be,
but I am not ready
to accept that fact yet…

We Are

We are all perfect
in our own
little imperfections.

We are loud, yet quiet.
we are broken, yet strong.
we are full, yet so empty.
we are hateful, yet loving.
we are full of life, yet act so dead.
we want to die, but we love life.
we are full of doubt, yet still confident.
we are aware, but act as we have no clue.
we are a blur, but we are more than we can ever imagine.

We are what we are,
how we are,
because,
we chose to be this way…

We Are

If you look closely, we are all we need,
with a little craziness and
someone to love, to finish the journey…

I need you…

I need us…

Left

How you feel doesn't matter.
It may to you, but not to anyone else.

The person you love
might be the world for you.
However,
you also have to understand
that who you love may or may not
love you back. You might be willing to
wait all your life,
but the truth is you don't have to.

You cut yourself open,
you put your heart out
for him/her to pick up.
All they did was turn away.
They left…

No one deserves that…

Collateral Damage

In the beginning,
all I wanted,
no,
needed,
no,
wished,
yes,
wished,
was that you look at me,
in a way that you feel
something too…

I know now,
no,
maybe,
no,
certain,
yes,
certain,
that it wasn't meant to be,
and I was just
collateral damage…

Life's Lesson

A lesson in life,
is that two negatives
make a positive.

We've all learnt this,
some of us remember,
for some, well, it's there
in the subconscious.

We are all so hung up onto
the negatives, that we forget
completely about positives.
Life has a way of correcting
itself, just remember that
this is where you belong
at the moment, right here…

So, live it out, enjoy and
let life give you the positive
moments in its time…

There

There…

Away from all the
judgments of the
world,

There…

In the midst of
foggy clarity of
explanations,

There…

Where nothing is
lost and all is
cherished,

There...

I wait for you
with the undying
hope that maybe,
maybe, we will have a
chance...

Regrets

Seeking you every hour of everyday,
I find myself estranged at the bay,
sometimes I am awake all night,
sometimes I am away all day…

He didn't say a word, he just left.
His heart was aching and he was drenched,
a fence around the heart quite high.
did you notice him, he doesn't smile…

A note left for her, asking to return,
consider the love he has to offer,
she didn't see him fit, or so he felt,
killed himself one night, finally dealt…

She returned one day hoping he waits,
saw his empty home and cobwebs,
all he asked was an indication to wait,
she suffocated, regretting her mistake…

Life Support II

It's not the oxygen I inhale,
or the water I drink,
or the things I feel,
or the wonders I see
that keeps me alive.

It's You.

See, you are what I breathe. Your fragrance,
And your laughter quenches my thirst.
I feel alive when I hold you in my arms
your touch gives me strength.
I don't want to see the wonders of this
world if you are not beside me.

You are my life support.
You have always been my life support.
You will always be my life support.

I guess you will never figure this out
by yourself.

I am afraid that you will never know…

What We Said

"It's too late now, we can't be together anymore",

I said, in a shaking voice.

"It's never too late if it feels right."

She answered, in a calming voice.

Morphine

What would the world be like? I used to imagine, of course, I was alone then, was not in love, but with a shattered soul and a pledge never to fall in love again.

Then, one day, she was just there standing right in front of me. I didn't know what hit me, because every bone in my body started to hurt. It hurts to breathe, talk, or walk in her absence. The pain just subsides when I see her, still there hurting, but mildly this time.

It's like this body of mine craves her touch. She has somehow become my morphine. She would learn in a couple of years that it's too late for me. I am as good as dead. She knew she could help.

Instead --

She left me to die.

What 'He' Craves

What he craves is a touch, touch of love.
What he craves is to show his scars to the world
and not be judged.
The blade marks that he covers on his wrist,
which no one noticed till date.
The bags under the eyes, which reveal that he hasn't
slept in days.
What he craves is a real connection to a soul,
not as complicated as his.

He looks at you and you ignore every time.
He craves for you, not in a psychopathic way,
but in a way like a child craves for the mother.
In a way like the ocean craves for the shore.
In a way like the earth craves for the sunlight,
and the waves of the sea for the moon.

He craves for you like a lover, guardian angel, and
the reliever, expecting to come out and speak in
front of the world, and you should know you are
his world. As long as you are okay with the fact

that he had problems, he will be okay. He craves for your understanding, because he craves you.

In his simple way, he loves you.

My Existence

He would always be present when needed.
He is un-noticed, but lurking in the corners.
No-one ever cared if he's present or not,
until, one day he didn't show up.
They found a note in his place, which said
"it's time."

They didn't make much sense of it then,
until three days later they decided to check
on him and knocked on his door.
He opened, they seemed relieved that he
was okay. Then they proceeded to ask,
"Why did you stop showing up?"
"It was time," he said.
"Time for?"
"To see if I existed for you all."

"And?"

After a brief pause he said ––

"You are three days late."

Road to You

This is the path I am on,
walking on dry leaves,
which sound like bones
breaking with every step
that I take towards you.

I hold a lantern in my
hand and I am afraid
to put it down, fearing
it may burn the only
road which leads to you.

What if?

Remember the ache in your heart,
which wants you to do something
You are never sure about it,
but hell, do it anyway.
It's as close as you'll get to pursue
your dreams.

If you ever decided to listen to
something, let this be it.
It's rarely wrong and you won't
have any regrets later for not doing it.

Trust me, not doing this will eventually
creep up on you with an only question,

"What if?"

Love at First Sight

I don't believe in love at first sight, there's nothing like it.

Love takes time, patience, and attention.

Love is not complete if you don't know someone. So, next time you feel that its love at first sight, remember that it only means that you would like to know the other person and may want to find out if they are the one.

That's all there is to it…

I Know

She looks into this void,
this emptiness,
trying to find a reason,
for the reasons,
that made her feel
the way she does.

She shouts into this void
with her highest pitch and
doesn't get any answer.
Rather the voice vanishes
without an echo and that
breaks her a little more
every time. However, you
will never know if she is fine
or broken because every time
you ask her, she is going to say
she's fine.

Then there are times
she doesn't answer and that's
when I know something is wrong.
That's when she knows that I know…

Sleeping Beauty

"Are we there yet?"

She asked, waking up startled,
on the front seat beside me.

"We've already crossed it five times."

I replied.

"Why didn't you wake me up then?"

She asked.

"You looked peaceful after a very longtime.

I didn't want to be the one to disturb that."

I replied, with a smile on my face.

"Can we make three more rounds?"

She asked.

And that's what I did, while she slept in peace.

Last Breath

I pulled her close to me,
held her at her waist
and kissed her mouth.

And when we parted
it was like I lost
my soul and that's the
last breath I took.

The Stranger in the Mirror

There's a stranger I see when I look in the mirror. I have known a different person, a person who laughed, a person who used to be present, and a person who used to make others smile, shared stories, and understood emotions.

Then I fell in love. Initially all the emotions increased exponentially, then there was the heartbreak, which made me who I am today. A person, who isn't interested in anyone's life, who wants to be left alone, who doesn't smile anymore, who isn't present and who doesn't care.

But once in a while the old me resurfaces and feels everything at once and I am afraid to go back to that again.

Ever…

I am a stranger to myself and I am traveling alone. That's not me in the mirror, that's the ghost I am afraid of…

One Day

"One day",
I said to her before we parted our ways.

She had asked,
"Will I ever see you again?"

Usually, people respond by sure or definitely.
I don't know
why I said,
"One day."

That was then, today, it all makes perfect sense.
'Someday' or 'Sure' or 'Definitely'
wasn't going to work here.
Luck had its paws buried deep in
our lives, which I couldn't see or realize.

I haven't seen her since,
but I hope I will – One Day.

Once in a Lifetime

And once in a while,
she reaches out,
not to say how she is,
but to know
if I am still surviving.

And once in a while,
I reach out,
not to say how I am
surviving, but to
see if she still responds.

And then,
there is a silence
we don't break…

A Memory in Description

We are here now, we could be anywhere, but we chose to be here, you and me in two different places, away from each other when we could have been together.

I can't say about you, but I miss you. I miss you in a way the sand misses the beach or lungs yearn for air. It's a life threatening feeling of losing you and I have no clue how to face this. You and I, at this moment are busy. You, with whatever you have to do, and I, with your memory. A vague face in mind trying to describe you in words and failing every time.

This is what it has finally come to. I always refer to 'us' as 'we' hoping there is a chance that one day we will find our way to each other. Until then, I will keep trying to describe you with some words of mine and hope it reaches perfection…

Broken II

You don't belong to me,
you never did.
What's really mine are these
broken pieces of myself.
I miss the way we used to
throw each other at the wall
when we made love.
That was exceptionally and
unrealistically amazing.
The feeling, sheer feeling
of you breathing on my neck
and biting to tease me, I miss that too.

And every time, I threw you,
or pushed you against the wall,
my eyes would open and
I am struck by reality.
You never let me make love
to you even in my dreams.
The reality is that
you don't belong to me.
You loved only him,
even in my dreams,
you belong to him…

Life's Journey

Life so far has been an eventful journey, made friends out of enemies, lost friends because of love. Bonded more with old friends and grew close with some new ones too.

I have faced the times of music, and lover's quarrels too. Seen children grow up, and some left us too soon. Failed to stand up sometimes, other times stood up too soon.

Loved a couple times and was called every time a fool. Won a losing battle, thought that was pretty cool. Mistakes of a father, why would the son be excused?

A mother hopes that her son won't become recluse. A sister hopes that her brother will be there with no excuse. What have I become, a poet for a muse? I wish she would've said once that we will be together too.

Life has become a battle of survival, people love only to use. Wars being fought for religion, did that become a religion too? All the questions that I have, hold an answer in them for sure.

We are fighting for land now; will we be fighting for oil too? Oh wait! I forgot, we've already done that too.

What's more left to see, I don't feel what you feel beneath the mask I wear, it's another mask I feel. The times I've felt laughter, was only to grow softer, a lesson I learnt was too hard, and I could never smile after. I survived two encounters with death and a couple after. Some might call that lucky and cool, I now feel like that should've been my exit, so today I wouldn't be the Greater Fool.

Broken Souls

We are all broken souls,
in one way or another.
We have these cracks in
our souls that illuminate
the surroundings in which
we are.

We look at each other and
wish to be that perfect as
the person next to us,
with them also wishing the same.

We are perfect for everyone
around us, until the time we
are ourselves.

And that just breaks my heart…

Nights as These

The silence we are sharing now,
has exceeded more than I had thought.
Do you ever think about me?
Sitting quietly, holding a book in your
hands, and the lights off.
Do you ever think that if we had
tried we could have pulled through?
Do you think all we need is to see
each other again, and may be all the
late night thoughts of 'what ifs?'
might get answered.

All I have with me at this hour,
this early hour at 4:35 in the morning
are questions, questions about you
having questions about us. I know
it's not possible, or maybe it is.
I don't need the questions.

Nights as These

I am searching for the answers.
If you are up to it, we can search for
them together. All you have to do is
reach out, you know, to the corner
where I live,

in your heart…

Losing it Finally

What's left of me is this piece of blank paper and no words to write on it. I already have far too many apologetic memoirs for you, to make you understand what you mean to me. I mean, that's not going to happen anymore.

Fuck you, and your late night thoughts, those voices in my head and dreams of you in my bed. I will stab each dream I saw to be with you with the very hands I have used to describe them in words, waking up from my warm bed in the middle of cold nights. The decaying thoughts of yours had their fun.

No more fucking romantic letters to tell you that I am still hung over the thought that you might one day return.

And when I fucking make up my mind that never again, all she does is call my name in that sweet tone of hers for me to lose track.

Fuck, there's no cure for this, is there?

Pain is the Fear

"And what do you know of love?" She asked.
After a pause, he said to her,
"Nothing, and that's the reason it's wonderful."
"And what do you know of pain?" She asked.
He didn't say anything for a while, then replied,
"Everything, and that's the reason I will never hurt you."

Seasons

She is like the seasons -- changes from time to time to what best fit her circumstances.

Sometimes, she shined like the summer sun, blinding everyone with her scorching beauty making everyone perspire when she entered the room.

Sometimes, she was like the spring, bringing smiles to everyone's face with her presence and giving them a reason to move on, hearing their stories and sharing hers to instill hope that it gets better eventually.

Sometimes, she cuts off herself from the crowd, responds in a way like the winter breeze cuts through your skin like a sharp knife, also apologetic at the same time with some dew drops to condition the pain caused, asking not to disturb her for some time and finds solace in the midst of fog. She was winter then, loved by all, but cold.

Sometimes, she couldn't hold it in any longer and finds herself under the clouds, with a slow drizzle under her eyes that just synchronizes with the rain falling from the sky.

Seasons

She never thought anyone might pay attention to this; however, there was someone who did, someone, who she wasn't paying any attention to…

The Push

He wanted to leave, she wanted him to stay.
"Long distance relationships rarely work," she said.

He stayed, love left.

New Year's Eve

The next time we cross each other's paths, let's not look away. Let's go on the journey which our eyes and bodies want to take us on. Let's not live for others and let's not be scared of what the world might say. Let's just be what we are destined to be.

You and I are complicated souls intertwined in the most complex of ways, unable to decipher the codes the universe has set for us. Let's not give the universe another day to smile at our fates.

Let's spend the night in bed together and wake up to the chirping of the birds, the sun rising to our foggy windows on a winter morning. Let your skin be on mine and feel my breath on your neck. Kiss me at the most unexpected of moments and let me make you blush with kisses on your neck.

All it takes is a glance. I am ready, let's be what we are meant to be. So, are you looking forward to this New Year's Eve?

The Healer

This is where the heart lies,
in the midst of empty lanes
leading to god knows what
mysterious place.

This is where I want to spend
the remaining days of my life,
in solace with your memory.
You and I remember each other
very differently.
For you I was the pain, and
for me you were the healer.

I had always wondered,
will it ever work, and finally
understood that the healer
always kills the pain.
And I returned every time
to die at your hands with a
smile on my face…

Love's Destruction

I met him the other day trying to find a purpose after you left, without saying what he had to do without you. He was lost. I spoke to him looking in his red, dead eyes, which of course were due to lack of sleep. He said he has lost the sense of pain, he doesn't feel it anymore. He doesn't care if anyone calls him names, he just keeps walking and talking about you. The world has started to call him a lunatic. He writes always and says you are his inspiration.

He moved away from his home to the mountains. She stays up there for days. He says he's trying to think it's time to live again, love again. Afraid, obviously of the consequences as he always gave too much of himself and never got anything in return. He wanted to talk to someone, to say that he is still in love with you. I don't know why he chose me to share his pain. I don't even talk to you yet here I am writing his words for you.

He took me to his cabin, where he gets away from the world trying to paint your picture in words. Looking at him made me question, how could such a beautiful thing as love become someone's destruction? This was the longest conversation I've had with him in years. I sat there looking at him while he wrote about you again. I wonder if his words will ever get to see the light of day. I wonder if you'll ever get to read them. We both sat there looking at each other in complete silence. I looked back up in the mirror, he was gone without even a word.

I wonder if he would survive.

Distant

And sometimes I just lie down on my bed
looking at the ceiling, thinking about her.
Thinking, what she must be doing at this
very hour, when I think of her.

Does she think of me too? A question I ask
myself every time, with her thought in mind.

I take my phone out of my pocket,
type everything I want to say to her
I type her name in the 'To:' field,
read it aloud and delete it.

That's the closest I get to say,
how much I love her.
That's how far I am from her.
That's how far I will always be
from her…

She Will be Loved

And sometimes,
she didn't care
if anyone loved her
or
hated her.

She knew,
she was worth it
and
the right man
will make the effort
to get her attention.

She knew
she will be
loved.

It's About Love

It was never about making her fall in love with me.
It was always about loving her no matter what I get in return.

That's how I had started loving her, being honest to the core, not knowing who she was, not knowing her secrets or her past. I never thought that would ever matter, but damn, I was wrong. It all connects in the end. Everything you do, things you hold onto, you let go every miniscule detail I have put down on paper about her smile. Every curve of her body I could never touch, waking up in the middle of every night crying, hoping, wishing her to be with me, praying, with a cigarette in between my lips. Never really thought it would eventually come to this.

It was never about making her fall in love with me, it was always about falling in love with her all over again, every time I saw her.

It was always about love…

What He Had to Offer

She was going to get away. I knew it from the moment I laid my eyes on her. She had that fire burning in her that you wished you could put out by giving her a hug, but wouldn't consider the possibility that it may incinerate you in the process.

You would be willing to die for her, but all this doesn't matter. She had heard the sacrificing stories far too many times to believe them.

She didn't need someone to put off her fire. She wanted someone who would let it mold her into what she would eventually become when it all cools down. She just needed someone to be there to love her for what she is and what she would be. Love was the thing that mattered. Love was all I had to offer, but she never asked me what I had…

Do You Remember?

"Do you remember?" – I asked.
"What?" – She asked me.

"Everything," I said.

"The first time we met,
the way I fell in love with you,
the moments we spent together,
the promises we made, about forever,
me walking away after a quarrel,
you teaching me about morals,
you holding a knife at your wrist,
me punching the walls with my fist,
you pass right by me,
I stopped, hoping you would find me,
us talking out of everyone's sight,
fighting to stay together with all our might,
we get married, live on a hilltop,
you say in the morning, the wall clock stopped.
The life we lived together is somewhat blurry,
do you remember honey, our life's journey?"

Do You Remember?

"None of that ever happened" – She said.

"You do remember then,
what we've missed."

Unclaimed Love

It has been two years. Two years since I stood in front of her and told her that I love her. Two years since she had said "no" without letting me complete what I had to say, two years of passing in the hallways trying to catch a glimpse of her face. Two years of carrying around this unrequited love, roaming, half-dead, walking wounded with a smile on my face, trying to hide the damage from the world, clinging on to this hopeless rope, which burns, and, I have no clue if she would catch me. Two years of sleepless nights and lonely mornings. Two years of love lost, for the only reason that I loved.

Two years have passed, in the hope that one day she would let me complete what I had to say. Two years of unbearable pain, greater than what death would inflict as she stands at arm's length from me but will never be in these arms. Countless hours in these two years spent silently waiting for her to show up. Two years' worth of scribbled pages, written to tell her, I just can't get over her. It took me two years to realize that this will last forever, and that she will not be a part of me, ever.

Two years I kept these words with me, now I hand them over to her, as they are rightfully hers. They always were.

Unclaimed Love

Two years ago, this was left midway, "I love you, and I want to marry you. I don't want you for your beauty, I love your soul and that's what I need. I don't want you, I need you. I know you don't know me too well, and I know you like to explore things and I do too and if you say 'yes' today, we can explore each other for the rest of our lives together."

Two years ago, you walked away. For the last two years, I have loved you every single day.

The Pull

Sometime I sit back and think about all the things we couldn't do and try to understand why we couldn't make it.

I know the only answer I will find is one of us didn't fight hard enough to be together and there's nothing that can be done about it now, because it's too late.

I can't roam in the cold dreaded winters anymore with the thought that you will eventually come one day. It's time for me to let go. Let it all go, and cut the cord that keeps bringing me back to you when you stretch your arms in the morning.

What Love Is?

"I finally figured out the reason
we end up alone.
It's not the person we fall in love with
when we do,
we fall in love with love itself.

And I've never heard a happy ending
to a story where
a mortal falls in love with something
as powerful and immortal
as love and survive."

Within Me

Within me, somehow your name
got etched onto the white blood cells,
they know now
that every time I think of you
I become sad.

The first thing they do is
fight back and attack each other.
What they don't realize is,
they are killing me a little more
in the process.

You've turned the system
that's meant to protect me,
against me.

You rule me now,
not from afar,

but from
within me…

Hope

"Time flies, relationships end.
People learn, sometimes they let go,
sometimes they hold on.
They don't know yet they are
holding onto disappointments.
They don't know yet that
it's all for nothing.

But if it gives a dying man
hope to expect something
better from tomorrow,
who are we to take that away?"

Almost

Its time you left this broken house of mine.
I've spent more time in repairing this heart,
than you've actually stayed in it.

And every time you leave, your heels puncture
my heart, almost killing me.

Almost...

Mine

She took me closer to the Devil's trap and reined the fire onto me, she was not my salvation, but turned out to be my annihilation. She made maps to her location using the veins of my body, making me addicted to study her astronomy. She would linger in the shadows to pick me up when I fall, she would feed on my fears so she could stand tall. She gave me reasons to fight back every morning; she never did leave the door as others did storming. She believed in me, but never did she love me, she was the story in a story that never came with a warning. She was the high of the tide at the lowest point, and made me feel low with her absence at the highest. She wasn't true to herself and nor was I, we might have been together if we had not asked questions such as why.

Is it not enough to say that I love you? Is it not enough to say I will be your beginning and your end? She doesn't say a word in the quietest moments of my life; she wants me to find her voice while we are drowning. She came close to me and I named her my queen as her soft lips whispered, you now belong to me…

Warm You Up

All I want is
to be that blanket
that you pull up
to wrap yourself
in the middle
of the night,
when a cold breeze of air
wakes you up
during winter.

Questions as These

I've woken up
to every single day
there is.

Tell me,
when will I
wake up to you?

Blurry

Somewhere
between the
thin lines of
reality and
fiction,
honesty and
deception,
I scribble
my thoughts
onto paper.

The fiction is that
I write you
with me
in my tales
and honestly
I am just
deceiving
myself.

Last Will

One day I will be gone, just like everyone else. There's an envelope that contains letters that I've written addressed to her, which one of you might stumble upon.

When that happens, don't let anyone read them. Don't read it. Don't try to find her to give them those letters; she will just throw them away. Instead, burn them, for I've been on fire since the day I saw her and I'm certain the screams from the flames will tell you everything you need to know, with a bizarre sense of warmth that rises from the flames.

In that moment, when there's nothing more left to burn, and my final words turn into ashes, I will know, she never came looking for them.

III

The End Begins

Silence

Do you hear that?
The sound of sheer silence between us?
That's our dream shattering.

Always

Always is never enough,
it has to be more,
forever maybe…

Scattered

I lie scattered, like pieces of glass
bearing a cut every time I try to piece
myself together…

I know now, that these imperfections
are perfect and make me who I am…

Cold

My soul has gone cold,
it needs fire to feel again,
I need you to light me up…

May Be

Maybe, just maybe, you think of me,
and that's what makes my pen
write your name every time…

Universes

At this very moment,
in a parallel universe we are together,
and that's comforting…

Hold This Heart

Hold onto this heart for me,
I know it's too bloody
with a lot of scars,
but that's all I have,
don't let it slip away, please!

Drowned

It drowned me completely,
it came in waves, high and low
love like a Tsunami.

Tripping

Do you not see me
tripping every single time
falling for you?

Journey

When I started, I had no clue what this journey was going to seem like.
Now after a thousand scribbled pages and some sensible poetry,
I feel that this was either to get close to you or move away from you forever.

That my dear, is a closure I am still seeking…

Death

I die every day,
only to wake up lonely.
Death actually isn't the end.

Waiting

Sorry to say this,
but it's time for me to move on.
Are you coming?

Porcelain Snow

This year's snow
leaves scars on my palms.
It doesn't melt
the way it used to.

This year,
it's porcelain snow,
which pricks
every memory of you
every time it falls on me.

Unleash the Soul

The wounds have healed completely.
Now, what remains are these
scars and the stories of their origin.

The eyes are sad and the lips hold
a convincing smile. The eyes are red and
the hands trembling for a touch.

It finds an unhealed wound that
tried to escape, just to tell the world
its wild story of love, life, and hate.

But, above all else, is its survival.

The soul wants to be heard…

No Way Back

The bridge is crossed.
Bonds are broken.
Lines are drawn.
Do not be mistaken,
what you left
on the other side
will come to haunt you
in your darkest nights
and cold winter mornings.
Once this match is lit
and the bridge is burnt,
the ashes you will breathe would be
of memories happy and sad,
of people alive and dead, or
of love lost and unspoken of.
Once this bridge turns to ash
you ought to know
there's absolutely
No Way Back…

Jar of Regrets

I have my fair share of regrets, like
a jar I carry around everywhere I go.
I call it 'Jar of Regrets'.

In this jar, there are
broken promises, hateful words,
jealousy, lost relationships,
tethered friendships,
unrequited love stories,
and their dreadful endings.

There's also stories of broken trust,
sleepless nights, missed kisses, and sacrifice.

This jar is a reminder of the storms
I've been through. This jar,
I call a 'Jar of Regrets' has been
getting me ready to lead a life without you.

Renaissance

What if everything that's happening
has already happened?
What if the present has repeatedly
repeated itself and we are
just trying to get it right?
What if this is the Renaissance?

Revival

My bones snap,
blood oozes out of my veins,
skin burned and my sins
beg for forgiveness.
I can't breathe,
a hand reaches
out of flames,
a phoenix,
breathes into my
smoke filled lungs,
giving me another chance
at redemption, at life.
I'm revived by love,
a love I can never have.

The House I Was Born

I was born an empty shell
with a heart protected by a ribcage.
And, one day everything I was
in me, slowly started to disappear.
She took over the furniture,
the heart was hers,
and now she remains protected
underneath the ribcage,
protecting me from inside.
Until one day, she left.
Leaving this house
we built, in a ruin
to be awed by onlookers.
But nobody wanting
to make it theirs again.
The house I was born was left
an empty shell, again.

Starting Anew

Everything ended eventually. That's all you need to know, you'll have another chance to start anew. And, if you are clever enough you'll realize it could be this moment.

Stumble

31 Years ago,
I was born.

30 years ago,
I learnt to walk.

Today,
I Still Stumble…

12:45 (08-05-2019)

Life, like many before me had said, doesn't come with a manual. You steer it left and right with a hope you find your purpose and probably fulfill it. You may hit a bump here and there, fly for a while, and fall flat on your face.

Life is not about being careful at every step, but stepping into the unknown with an open mind, learning to duck when things fly at you and knowing when to put yourself in front of the things that matter.

I end this here at 12:45 AM, a chapter in my life I had started a couple of years ago. I've found love, that's crazy, frightful, and oh so innocent. I have a son now, and he obviously takes after his mother. I never thought I would have this, ever, in my life. The decisions I have made, the mistakes I keep making, and the fights I keep picking, I am surprised I lasted this long.

Life… It's great to have something unknown in front you, like a mystery. Events unfolding every second, no idea where the next set of events unfold that just get tied up in your life accidentally or maybe because of something you've done along the way. Life will always twist it until

12:45 (08-05-2019)

the very end, a thriller, suspense, riddled life. There's always more to it.

More than love…

About the Author

Mohammed Abrar Ahmed is the author behind @thficklepoet. He has earlier published a chapbook ***The Years Gone By***, and this is his second attempt to get his words out on a worldwide platform in his first-ever full book. When he is not writing, he is usually dreaming about writing and by the time he gets to it, well, he's not writing. He has been an analyst, a project manager, an Urdu poet, and even a comedian and he's currently looking for a job. For the time being, he's living in London, Ontario with his wife and their son.

You can connect with me on:
- https://www.twitter.com/theficklepoet
- https://www.facebook.com/theficklepoet
- https://www.instagram.com/theficklepoet

www.ingramcontent.com/pod-product-compliance
Lightning Source LLC
Chambersburg PA
CBHW070426010526
44118CB00014B/1923